CENGAGE Learning

Drama for Students, Volume 21

Project Editor: Anne Marie Hacht

Editorial: Michelle Kazensky, Ira Mark Milne, Timothy Sisler **Rights Acquisition and Management**: Margaret Abendroth, Edna Hedblad, Jacqueline Key, Mari Masalin-Cooper **Manufacturing**: Rhonda Williams

Imaging: Lezlie Light, Mike Logusz, Kelly A. Quin **Product Design**: Pamela A. E. Galbreath

Product Manager: Meggin Condino

For more information, contact
Gale, an imprint of Cengage Learning
27500 Drake Rd.
Farmington Hills, MI 48331-3535
Or you can visit our Internet site at

individual does not imply endorsement of the editors or publisher. Errors brought to the attention of the publisher and verified to the satisfaction of the publisher will be corrected in future editions.

ISBN 0-7876-6818-4
ISSN 1094-9232

Printed in the United States of America
10 9 8 7 6 5 4 3 2 1

An Ideal Husband

Oscar Wilde

1895

Introduction

An Ideal Husband premiered in London, England, on January 3, 1895, and was published in 1896. It was the third of Wilde's four comedic plays to be staged, and it was as big a success with audiences as the previous two. However, critics of the time were not as appreciative as audiences, which was the case for all of Wilde's social comedies. Critics thought these plays more flippant than substantive; audiences were delighted by the wonderful wit of the dramas. Numerous choice "one-liners" and other pithy witticisms that Wilde's dramatic characters deliver are still quoted by people today.

An Ideal Husband is often called a "social comedy" because it has both a serious ("social") as well comedic plot line. On the one hand, the play is about a prominent politician who is in danger of losing his reputation as a paragon of integrity, owing to a youthful indiscretion that the play's villain is threatening to expose. Although the politician's transgression is not exposed, this plot line conveys the idea that there are very few people in the world who are wholly good and to pretend so is hypocritical. This is a message for Wilde's contemporaries, a late-Victorian group obsessed with purity and goodness but, of course, as imperfect as the people of any other age. On the other hand, the play is supposed to be funny, as it is, thanks to the witty bantering of the characters, especially in moments when the play is not directly concerned with the "social" plot.

Wilde and his play are by now firmly established in the English-language canon of literature, and most libraries hold volumes of the individual or collected plays. The Modern Library editions of Wilde's collected comedies are the most widespread.

Author Biography

The writer and wit known as Oscar Wilde was born Oscar Fingal O'Flahertie Wills Wilde in Dublin, Ireland, on October 16, 1854. This lavish and romantic set of given names evokes Irish myth and heroes, conveying Wilde's parents' pride in their Irish nationality.

Wilde came from a prominent family. His father, a surgeon who operated on the monarchs of Europe, was knighted. His mother, a historian and political commentator and activist, was very prominent in the Irish freedom movements that would bring Ireland its independence from England in 1921. Both of Wilde's parents published numerous books in their lifetimes.

As a boy in school, Wilde excelled in his favorite subjects. He then spent three years at Trinity College, one of the foremost universities in Ireland. He excelled at Trinity and then made his way to Oxford University in Cambridge, England. At Oxford he distinguished himself yet again, winning prestigious prizes.

Once he had graduated and established himself in London, Wilde began publishing in various genres: poetry, drama, essays, fairy tales, and more. He was also an editor of magazines. Equally important was the fame he gained in London as a wit and a dandy (someone devoted to fashion and style). In the midst of late-Victorian England's drably coated men, Wilde went about in knee breeches, fine vests, and long hair (at least for a time). He would speak at public events and art exhibits, and people would listen, vastly amused and intrigued. The magazines that chronicled the goings on about town in London began to satirize and parody Wilde. In 1894, Wilde married; he and his wife had two sons.

Wilde reached his pinnacle of fame in 1895, when *An Ideal Husband* premiered on the London stage. The Prince of Wales and many other notables were present on opening night and found the play very much to their liking. *An Ideal Husband* was the third of four highly successful plays Wilde wrote before his career was destroyed by an unfortunate and tragic turn of events.

Very shortly after the premieres of *An Ideal Husband* and Wilde's fourth comedic play, *The Importance of Being Earnest*, Wilde was found guilty of indecency and sentenced to two years in prison at hard labor. Wilde's trial followed his having charged a British aristocrat with libel for accusing him of homosexual acts—a mistake because Wilde was indeed involved with Sir Alfred Douglas at the time, and late-Victorian society was singularly intolerant of such free behavior.

After prison, his career and health ruined, Wilde lived his last days in France. He died on November 30, 1900, in Paris. In 1909, his remains were moved to the French National Cemetery of Père Lachaise. His last major works are *De Profundis* and *Ballad of Reading Goal*, both of which pertain to his terrible trial and imprisonment.

Plot Summary

Act 1

The action of *An Ideal Husband* takes place within about twenty four hours. Act 1 takes place at Sir Robert Chiltern's house, which is located in the fashionable part of London. The Chilterns are hosting a reception. The first two speakers of the play, two minor characters, Lady Basildon and Mrs. Marchmont, set a witty tone. They are pretty, young married women, and they speak to each other languidly and cleverly. Attention then moves to various new arrivals at the reception, such as the Earl of Caversham, who inquires after his son Lord Goring, and Mabel Chiltern, Sir Robert Chiltern's sister, who chats with the Earl of Caversham. The most important arrivals, however, are Lady Markby and Mrs. Cheveley, because the latter is the play's villain.

That something serious will be occurring in this otherwise comic play becomes clear when Lady Markby introduces Mrs. Cheveley to Lady Chiltern. Lady Chiltern realizes that she knows Mrs. Cheveley, but under a different name—the name of her first husband. Mrs. Cheveley clearly disturbs Lady Chiltern, and Lady Chiltern appears to dislike the other woman intensely.

Mrs. Cheveley has come to the party to speak to Sir Robert specifically, and, soon enough, the two find themselves alone. What she wishes to talk about is blackmail: if Sir Robert does not support what is in fact a doomed South American canal scheme in a speech to the parliament the next day, she will reveal the terrible secret of his youth, which will destroy his life and career. Shaken to his core, Sir Robert agrees to do her bidding.

At the end of act 1, Lady Chiltern succeeds in getting her husband to admit that Mrs. Cheveley has persuaded him to change his mind about the canal project. She is outraged and convinces her husband to write to Mrs. Cheveley immediately, telling her that he will not support the project in his parliamentary speech. Wondering what kind of power Mrs. Cheveley has over her husband, Lady Chiltern declares that it had better not be blackmail —that he better not be one of those men who pretend to be pillars of the community but who in fact have shameful secrets.

Act 2

Act 2 opens the next morning, once again at the Chiltern residence. Lord Goring and Robert Chiltern are speaking; Chiltern is telling his good friend Goring everything. At one point, Chiltern bitterly wonders why a youthful folly has the power to ruin a man's career, even when that man has spent so many years doing good works. To this Goring replies that what Chiltern did was not folly but fairly ugly and very grave: he sold a state secret for money.

Chiltern tries to explain, saying that when he was young he was poor, so that it did not matter that he came from a good family because his prospects were limited by a lack of funds. He tells how he was seduced by the teachings of Baron Arnheim, who turned his head with "the most terrible of all philosophies, the philosophy of power." The baron "preached to [him] the most marvelous of all gospel, the gospel of gold," he says. Chiltern says he was ferociously ambitious, and that when the chance came to make his fortune, it did not matter that it depended on a crime; he took it.

Lady Chiltern comes home while the men are conversing. She has been at a "Woman's Liberal Association" meeting, where, as she says, they discuss things such as "Factory Acts, Female Inspectors, the Eight Hours Bill, the Parliamentary Franchise," and so on. Soon, Robert Chiltern leaves and Mabel Chiltern takes his place, asking Goring if he will meet her the next morning. Goring agrees and then leaves. Next, Lady Markby and Mrs. Cheveley are announced. Mrs. Cheveley is inquiring about a diamond broach she lost the day before, asking whether it was found by anyone at the reception. (Lord Goring found the broach and still has it.)

When Lady Markby leaves, Lady Chiltern and Mrs. Cheveley are able to speak to each other frankly. Lady Chiltern makes it clear that Mrs. Cheveley is not welcome in her house. This spurs Mrs. Cheveley to tell Lady Chiltern the truth about her husband, and she warns Lady Chiltern that she will carry out her threat. Lady Chiltern is devastated to find out that her husband is like so many other men, men who have shameful secrets. She confronts her husband and tells him that her love for him is dead.

Act 3

Act 3 takes place in Lord Goring's house, in the library, which is connected to a number of other rooms. Lord Goring is preparing to go out for the evening when he receives a letter from Lady Chiltern. It reads, "I want you. I trust you. I am coming to you." Goring rightly deduces that Lady Chiltern now knows the truth about her husband and that she needs to talk to someone.

Goring cancels his plans to go out and realizes that he must tell his servants that he is not in for anyone except Lady Chiltern; it would be disastrous for her reputation if she were found in his home without a chaperon. However, before he can do this, his father is announced. Unfortunately for Goring, his father is in the mood to lecture him. Goring tries unsuccessfully to get rid of his father and must listen to him go on about Goring's need to marry and settle down. In the meantime, Mrs. Cheveley has arrived, and a servant, thinking she is Lady Chiltern, escorts her into Goring's drawing room.

Finally able to show his father the door, Goring is put out to find Sir Robert Chiltern on his doorstep. Goring tries to get rid of Chiltern, believing all the while that Lady Chiltern is in the next room. He is concerned that Chiltern will discover his wife and misconstrue her presence in his home. Chiltern lingers and eventually overhears a sound coming from the room in which Mrs. Cheveley is waiting. He goes in, sees the woman, and returns to Goring disgusted. He believes that Mrs. Cheveley and Goring are having an affair. Goring, for his part, believes that Chiltern has just seen his own wife. Chiltern leaves and Goring sees that it is Mrs. Cheveley who is in the room.

Lord Goring has Mrs. Cheveley's diamond broach and tells her that the broach was a gift he gave to his niece, so that the only way Mrs. Cheveley could have come by it was to have stolen it, which she did. He threatens to call the police and have her prosecuted for theft unless she drops her blackmail plans. She has no choice but to concede, and Goring makes her hand over the letter Chiltern wrote all those years ago. Goring burns the letter.

Act 4

Act 4 is the resolution of the play. It takes place in the morning room of the Chiltern residence, the same setting as act 2. Lord Goring finally realizes that Mabel Chiltern is the woman for him and proposes. Mabel is very happy, as is the visiting Earl of Caversham. Lady Chiltern has forgiven her husband but still believes he must give up public life. She thinks they should retire to the country. Lord Goring convinces her otherwise. He makes her see that her husband thrives on politics, and if she were to take that away from him, he would become bitter and disillusioned and their marriage would suffer. Lady Chiltern realizes that Goring is right and relents. Sir Robert is ecstatic.

Media Adaptations

- *An Ideal Husband* was made into a film by a British production in 1947. This film version was directed by Alexander Korda and starred Paulette Goddard as Mrs. Cheveley and Michael Wilding as Lord Goring.

- *An Ideal Husband* was adapted for television in Britain in 1969 as part of a "Play of the Month" series.

- Another British production made *An Ideal Husband* into a film 1998. This version was directed by

William Cartlidge and starred James Wilby as Sir Robert Chiltern, Sadie Frost as Mrs. Cheveley, and Jonathan Firth as Lord Goring.

- A joint United States and Great Britain production of *An Ideal Husband* was made in 1999. This widely acclaimed version was directed by Oliver Parker and featured an all-star cast, including Cate Blanchett as Lady Gertrude Chiltern, Minnie Driver as Mabel Chiltern, Julianne Moore as Mrs. Cheveley, Jeremy Northern as Sir Robert Chiltern, and Rupert Everett as Lord Goring.

Lady Olivia Basildon

Lady Basildon and her close friend Mrs. Marchmont are the first speakers in Wilde's play, setting the tone with their witty banter. "They are types," Wilde's stage notes say, "of exquisite fragility," and they are female dandies. Lady Basildon and her friend affect a world-weary attitude, pretending to find the fashionable London parties they go to terribly boring. As Lady Basildon says of a different party the two are planning to attend: "Horribly tedious! Never know why I go. Never know why I go anywhere." The duo's worldly sophistication and wit undoubtedly flattered a portion of his audience whom Wilde hoped would enjoy his play, namely fashionable society women.

Lord Caversham

See Earl of Caversham

Mrs. Cheveley

Mrs. Cheveley, the villain of Wilde's play, enters the society of the Chilterns and Lord Goring determined either to get her own way or to destroy those who will not help her achieve her ends. She comes to London from Vienna, where she has been living for some time, to blackmail Sir Robert Chiltern. She knows Chiltern's terrible, scandalous secret and has concrete evidence of his transgression (a letter he wrote). She informs Chiltern that she will expose his sinful past unless he praises a South American canal scheme instead of condemning it for the stock market swindle it is as he plans to do in a parliamentary speech. Mrs. Cheveley and her friends have invested heavily in the scheme, and if the respected Chiltern were to advise his government to support it, Mrs. Cheveley and her friends would become much richer than they already are.

Since one of Wilde's points in the play is that large fortunes often have their roots in immorality, he needed to make Mrs. Cheveley's actions thoroughly unsympathetic to draw a convincing villain. The stock market manipulation had to be something that would not only increase her wealth but also eventually entail the impoverishment of others. Further, she is a blackmailer and habitual thief and liar. Still, this said, Mrs. Cheveley delivers some of the play's choicest witticisms.

Lady Gertrude Chiltern

Gertrude Chiltern is a sheltered, good woman who worships perfect goodness most especially in the form of her "ideal husband." The problem with her worship of perfection and of her husband is that her husband is not in fact perfect; indeed, he has an extremely disreputable secret in his past—a secret that could ruin his career.

Described as being possessed of "a grave Greek beauty," Lady Chiltern is appropriately noble in character. She is involved in all sorts of good works. For example, she is a feminist campaigning for the right of girls and women to have a higher education. She is, in short, a moneyed woman with principles: she believes that she must give something back to society by supporting charities, foundations, and other causes.

Lady Chiltern also believes that when women love men they worship them; by doing so, such women require that their men conform to their ideals of what is great. And until Lady Chiltern learns the truth about her husband's past, she is certain that he is indeed her ideal. She believes that he is a thoroughly good man committed to doing only good in the world.

Lady Chiltern must learn a stern lesson in the play: that nobody is perfect and that to wish this is naive and dangerous. Lady Chiltern, then, is not really perfectly good until she accepts the fact of, and is willing to forgive, imperfection.

Miss Mabel Chiltern

Mabel Chiltern has her eye on Lord Goring as a husband, and the two become engaged in the play's last act. She is the sister of Robert Chiltern. She is pretty, intelligent, and pert, and she is as witty as Lady Basildon and Mrs. Marchmont are. Knowing that Lord Goring is the man for her,

Mabel Chiltern is waiting gracefully and humorously, albeit somewhat impatiently, for him to realize that she is the perfect woman for him.

From Lord Goring's father's point of view, she is a clever and pleasing young woman who is far too good for the likes of his son. Mabel is a foil to Gertrude because she is a young woman who does not expect perfection from any human being. She declares that one of the reasons she likes Lord Goring is because he has faults.

Sir Robert Chiltern

A respected parliamentarian, Robert Chiltern is confronted by his disreputable past, blackmailed, and finally saved from any public scandal. The ugly secret of his past is that his fortune rests on his having sold a state secret. As a young man, he finds out that England intends to support an extensive overseas construction project, which means that anybody who invests in the project before the announcement is made public will become rich. In other words, whoever buys stock in the companies concerned before the prices of the stocks go up, on the strength of England's interest and support of the project, will reap a fortune.

Chiltern writes a letter to alert an acquaintance who buys a great deal of stock and pays Chiltern handsomely from the vast profits. Yet, what was required of the young Chiltern and all those in the know, as he knew very well, was strict secrecy and the ethical understanding that any "insider" stock purchases were criminal actions punishable by prison time.

Chiltern is horrified to learn that Mrs. Cheveley has the letter he wrote so long ago and plans to publish it unless he concedes to her demands. Ironically, what Mrs. Cheveley wants him to do is back an overseas construction project, so that, like Chiltern before her, she and her friends can make a financial killing on the strength of their early investments. The crucial difference, however, is that the scheme in which Mrs. Cheveley has invested is a scam, but Lord Chiltern's project was not.

Despite having planned to condemn the canal scheme because he knows that it is a scam, Chiltern capitulates to Mrs. Cheveley's demands. He cannot face scandal and ruin.

Chiltern changes his mind about his speech when his wife intervenes. Lady Chiltern knows the details of her husband's political activities and convinces him to deliver the speech he knows that he should. So, he writes a letter to Cheveley communicating his change of heart.

For a time, Chiltern is able to prevent his wife from finding out why Mrs. Cheveley has so much power over him, but eventually she discovers the truth. When she does, she declares that their love is dead. Chiltern is devastated, seeing his career and entire life crumbling around him. But, luckily for Chiltern, Lord Goring, his faithful friend, is able to foil Mrs. Cheveley's plans *and* convinces Lady

Chiltern that her husband still deserves her love.

Earl of Caversham

The Earl of Caversham (Lord Caversham) is Lord Goring's father, a stock characterization of a father who is perplexed by the vagaries of a son he simply cannot understand. He spends his time chastising his son and lecturing him about what he should do with his time. Short of doing something worthwhile with his life, Lord Caversham advises Lord Goring to marry at the very least. Clearly, despite his exasperation, Lord Caversham is fond of his lazy son.

Viscount Lord Arthur Goring

Lord Goring, a close friend of Sir Robert Chiltern, saves the day for his friend by foiling Mrs. Cheveley's blackmail attempt. He is able to prevent her from carrying out her threat because he acquires proof that she is a thief and tells her he will inform the police unless she drops her plan, which she does. Yet, Goring's involvement in the serious plot line of this play is far less entertaining than his involvement in the comedic goings-on of *An Ideal Husband*.

Lord Goring speaks the play's funniest lines, many of which are still quoted today. For example, he informs his butler Phipps that, "To love oneself is the beginning of a life-long romance, Phipps." He also has a funny rejoinder for his father when

Caversham says he cannot fathom how Goring can stand London society. According to Goring's father, London society has devolved into a "lot of damned nobodies talking about nothing." Goring replies: "I love talking about nothing, father. It is the only thing I know anything about."

Lord Goring is a dandy: he is not simply *in* fashion but *trendsetting* in dress; he pretends not to take anything seriously; he values witty repartee and excels at it.

If it were not for his father urging him to realize that it is time for him to marry, Lord Goring would undoubtedly continue in his life of perfect leisure and self-absorption. However, alerted to his duty to produce heirs, Goring opens his eyes and sees that the best companion for him as wife is close at hand in the person of Mabel Chiltern.

Mrs. Margaret Marchmont

Mrs. Marchmont is the friend of Lady Basildon. The two women are very close to each other and much the same in character.

Lady Markby

Lady Markby is Mrs. Cheveley's immediate connection to London society, as Mrs. Cheveley is younger and has traveled to London from Vienna alone. Lady Markby introduces Mrs. Cheveley to persons whom she does not yet know and chaperones the younger woman around town. She is an established, well-liked, older member of the moneyed, aristocratic society depicted in Wilde's play.

Phipps

Phipps is Lord Goring's "ideal" butler. Phipps is self-effacing and discreet. His job is not to assert himself or his own personality in any way. Yet, in conversation with Lord Goring, he is not above subtle humor—delivered quite impassively, however.

Vicomte de Nanjac

The vicomte is a French attaché who adores all things English and at whom Lord Goring pokes fun. His purpose in the play appears to be to have given the English audiences of the time something French to snicker at. This is a very popular gesture on Wilde's part, since the French and the English were involved in bitter political and cultural rivalries for a long time.

Themes

Scandal, Hypocrisy, and the Ideal

Cautioning Sir Robert that she will indeed carry out her threat and ruin his career, Mrs. Cheveley declares:

> Remember to what point your Puritanism in England has brought you. In old days nobody pretended to be a bit better than his neighbors. Nowadays, with our modern mania for morality, everyone has to pose as a paragon of purity, incorruptibility, and all the other seven deadly virtues —and what is the result? You all go over like ninepins—one after the other. Not a year passes in England without somebody disappearing. Scandals used to lend charm, or at least interest, to a man—now they crush him. And yours is a very nasty scandal. You couldn't survive it.

Here, in a nutshell, is the central message of Wilde's play: the more a culture upholds stringent moral values, the more likely it is that publicly prominent people will crumble under charges of impropriety. By this Wilde does not mean that immorality or criminal behavior is acceptable. What he means is that an exaggerated attachment to moral purity leads to social ills and not social good. This might seem counterintuitive; after all, should not the respect for moral purity lead to more people being truly good? For Wilde, it just leads to more people being failures in their own eyes and others' because it is impossible for most people not to make a mistake at some point in their lives. It encourages people not to hide even their minor vices, but to proclaim loudly against any and all weakness, thereby becoming hypocrites and paving the way for their greater shame if they are ever found out for their true selves. As Mrs. Cheveley's speech makes clear, in the Victorian climate of intolerance, politicians and other social leaders were pressured to proclaim themselves paragons of purity when they were not. Consequently, when the truth of their large or small sins came to the surface, their careers and reputations were compromised or ruined.

Mrs. Cheveley's speech was not only meant for Wilde's British audiences but also for his avid American audiences. This is not simply because America was culturally close to England but also because of pertinent American history and its continuing influence on American life. Some of the first Europeans to settle in the United States were members of Puritan sects, and what these Christian fundamentalists are most remembered for is their period of hysteria and cruelty. In their pursuit of moral purity they saw evil everywhere, declared numerous persons witches, and burned them alive (the "witch trials"). Extremism, in other words, leads only and always to tragedy, even if it is extremism in the name of good.

As far as Mrs. Cheveley is concerned, politicians who conform and project themselves as paragons of good are hypocrites. They, like Chiltern, have things they need to hide, whether in their past or in their present. Wilde's disdain for hypocrisy explains his attachment to characters who are dandies like Lord Goring. Lord Goring's dandy pose entails, essentially, the notion that he is wicked and cares about himself first of all. In other words, the values he professes are precisely the opposite of those who proclaim themselves upstanding citizens wedded to duty and the welfare of others. Yet, if the upstanding citizen cannot possibly be the paragon he or she professes to be, then he or she is akin to Goring—a person who will, at times, let his or her own interests take precedence over the public good. In short, says Wilde, it is better to be a Goring, who does not pretend to be good, than to be a hypocrite.

An Ideal Husband's play on things "ideal" or pure is related to its cautionary message about the Victorian obsession with perfect goodness. Obviously, the perfect specimen of any given thing is an ideal specimen of the thing. Lady Chiltern wants an ideal husband, which is a man who fulfills his husbandly role perfectly and who is, as well, an ideal human, i.e., perfectly good. She thinks this is what she has in Sir Robert, and Sir Robert, for his part, loves his wife so much that this is what he wants her to think. In learning that she is wrong to want such a thing, Lady Chiltern's development over the course of the play is a crucial component of the play's message.

The coupling of Mabel Chiltern and Lord Goring is Wilde's antidote to the Chilterns. Mabel, notably, declares that she wants to be a "good" wife to Lord Goring, not a perfect or ideal one. Lord Goring, perhaps, is Wilde's version of a good-enough husband, as he readily admits that he has faults. The human race, Wilde seems to say, will always fall short of its ideals, but this should not be occasion for tragedy. On the contrary, what leads to tragedy is insisting that perfection must be achieved even after the best that can be done has been tried.

Ambition

Politicians in late-nineteenth-century England were not terribly different from politicians today. They saw themselves as public servants and entered into politics to do some good and make a difference. Yet, to go far in politics it takes ambition. Politicians who aim to reach high positions in the government have to have nerves of steel and very thick skins. They are ruthlessly attacked by members of the opposing party; even others in their own party will attempt to outmaneuver them; journalists will dig into their private lives and print anything that will sell a magazine or newspaper; and so forth. Thus, in addition to wanting to do good, a politician aiming for the top has to be very ambitious. He or she has to have some craving for glory that makes all the pain of getting to the top bearable. In the ferociously ambitious Sir Robert Chiltern, Wilde presents just this type of politician. In doing so, he has presented his highly successful politician accurately. After all, Chiltern is only forty but he is already an under-secretary, and, at the end of the play, the prime minister offers him a cabinet position.

This depiction of the politician's hungry ambition makes sense in *An Ideal Husband*. The play is concerned with having people adopt a realistic view of the world and how it works; consequently, Wilde avoids an idealized picture of the motivations of top-ranking politicians.

Topics for Further Study

- Research the circumstances surrounding Oscar Wilde's trial and imprisonment.

- The two years Wilde spent in prison ruined his health. Late-nineteenth-century prison conditions were harsh and hard labor as a punishment was common. Research prisons and the treatment of prisoners in England from 1890, plotting the major prison reforms of the twentieth century.

- Research Wilde's mother, Lady Jane Francesca Wilde, née Elgee. What works of literature did she publish under her own name? What did she publish under the pen name "Speranza," and what was her role as a political writer in the cause of Irish independence?

- Research the major Irish uprisings against British rule in the late nineteenth and early twentieth centuries. Explore, for example, the Easter Uprising of 1916.

- Research the history of the Irish Republican Army (IRA). Are they freedom fighters, or terrorists, in your view?

- Study one or two plays by the eighteenth-century-British playwright William Congreve, a master of the comedy of manners. Compare one of the plays to Wilde's *An Ideal Husband* or *The Importance of Being Earnest*.

- Wilde's father Sir William Wilde was an aural surgeon and oculist known throughout Europe for his expertise. What was the science of ears and eyes of the time? How successful were the operations of eye and ear surgeons then compared to today? Who were some of Sir William's most well-known patients?

- Wilde's mother was an active feminist, besides being an Irish patriot. Investigate her feminist activities and the activities of feminists of the time.

Wit

Wit as a type of humor is what Wilde is known for, both in his everyday life and in a number of his writings, including *An Ideal Husband*. Wit is clever humor—not bawdy, rude, silly, or visual funniness. Wit entails the delivery of an unexpected or surprising insight, or a clever reversal of expectations. For example, at one point in the play, Mrs. Cheveley says, "a woman's first duty in life is to her dressmaker, isn't it? What the second duty is, no one has yet discovered." This would have provoked laughter because the popular saying she is reversing is as follows: "A woman's first duty is to her husband." Victorians were known for their commitment to duty and there would have been not one person in Wilde's audience who had not heard and read the popular axiom many, many times.

Epigram and Aphorism

Epigrammatic turns of speech are short and sweet, and they are somehow surprising or witty. Wilde's characters' wit is often epigrammatic. For example, as Mrs. Cheveley says at one point, "Oh! I don't care about the London season! It is too matrimonial. People are either hunting for husbands, or hiding from them." Mrs. Cheveley's purported reason for disliking the London social season is funny. Even funnier is that what makes the season "matrimonial" is not simply the search for husbands.

An aphorism is a brief statement containing an opinion or general truth, which might or might not be witty. Wilde excelled in wit in the form of aphorisms. Lady Cheveley, for example, delivers quite a few aphoristic witticisms in *An Ideal Husband*. For example, "Morality," she says, "is simply the attitude we take toward people whom we personally dislike." Or, as she says elsewhere: "Questions are never indiscreet. Answers sometimes are." There is also Lord Goring's opinion about good advice. In reply to Mabel Chiltern when she questions his having told her it's past her bedtime, Lord Goring says, "My father told me to go to bed an hour ago. I don't see why I shouldn't give you the same advice. I always pass on good advice. It is the only thing to do with it. It is never any use to oneself."

Comedy of Manners

While Wilde has a serious plot and message in *An Ideal Husband*, the play is mostly comic. As such, it is close to a form of dramatic comedy known as the comedy of manners. Comedies of manners are mostly associated with eighteenth-century Europe, although they date back to the beginnings of European drama. A comedy of manners is a play whose purpose is to satirize human vagaries. They focus on a particular stratum of society and make fun of that group's pettiness, hypocrisies, vanities, failings, and so forth. In *An Ideal Husband*, for example, Wilde satirizes the hypocrisy of the English ruling classes through his portrait of Sir Robert Chiltern. Comedies of manners are also characterized by their wit, i.e., the way that the characters' dialogue is composed mostly of clever and funny bantering. This explains Wilde's attraction to the form.

Melodrama

Melodramas tell their stories through sensational and improbable characters and turns of event. For example, villains are thoroughly villainous in melodrama, and heroes and heroines are purity itself. Rings, letters, gloves and such items are lost and found in ways that lead to all sorts of revelations and complications of plot. Heroines often end up in terrible danger, but the hero always arrives at the last moment to save the day, and so forth. Wilde employs some stock melodramatic situations and events in *An Ideal Husband*. For example, the detail of the incriminating letter from the past and the blackmail scheme on which the plot turns are melodramatic flourishes.

Problem Play

What are called problem plays were first written in Europe in the late nineteenth century. They are called this because they tackle some pressing social development of the day. For example, the playwright credited with introducing the form in its purest, earliest form is Henrik Ibsen, whose *A Doll's House* took on the issue of feminism: the struggles of Europe's "new" women and their families. If critics have difficulty calling *An Ideal Husband* a comedy of manners, and some prefer the term "social comedy," this is because the play has a serious element to it. This serious component reflects Wilde's respect for the problem play.

The Dandy

Dandies, of which there are many in Wilde's play, are a phenomenon of nineteenth-and early-twentieth-century Europe. Dandies were men that were known for their commitment to fashion—usually extravagant fashion—and for their love of all things beautiful in general. Nineteenth-century dandies in the new mega-cities such as, Paris, London, and New York, would stroll elegantly down pedestrian boulevards and frequent fashionable places. It is said that their exquisite nature and distaste for all things rough and vulgar stemmed from their dismay over a changing world. Specifically, these city dandies were witnessing the industrialization of their environment. This involved a change from a world where rural living was dominant to a world where factories in new urban centers were being rapidly built—with all their belching, polluting coal smoke, as well as their horribly exploited and impoverished workers (ten–twelve hour or more workdays, pitifully inadequate pay, and six, sometimes seven-day work weeks). What they saw was ugliness and the worship of money no matter the environmental and human cost, so they rejected the practical and spoke for the value of the ephemeral, the delicate, and the beautiful. It was a way of insisting that the creation of wealth was evil if the quality of peoples' lives was the price.

Wilde himself was a dandy in dress for some time. After graduating from Oxford, he spent a few years dressing in what was then considered exquisite fashion when he went out in the evenings. He did not go so far as to dress unusually in the daytime, however.

Many photographs of Wilde in one of his "exquisite" outfits exist; and what was so outrageous then were knee breeches and a velvet waistcoat, a flowing cloak, and longish hair.

Wilde did not dress unusually for his evenings out for long; as soon as he became well known he conformed, albeit always fashionably, to the more conservative tastes of the time.

Compare & Contrast

- **1890s:** Dandies dress themselves in clothes reminiscent of days gone by; some carry a single flower as an accessory.

  Today: A wide range of distinctive clothing that indicates a particular subculture, such as punk, Goth, and hip-hop, can be seen on the street of a typical American city.

- **1890s:** Conservative Victorian ideology still rules the day, despite a new generation's sense that it is becoming "modern."

Today: Alternative lifestyles and a general tolerance of difference coexists in the United States.

- **1890s:** Oscar Wilde's career was destroyed thanks to allegations of same-sex love affairs.

  Today: Same-sex marriage is legal in some countries, such as Canada; a debate over whether or not to institute state-sanctioned same-sex marriage is current in the United States.

- **1890s:** Queen Victoria, who gave the Victorian era its name, is known as the Imperial Queen; she declares herself Empress of India and Britain's world empire becomes vast.

  Today: The last of the British empire unravels in the mid twentieth century, and major British cities, such as London, are post-colonial, multi-ethnic metropolises.

Aestheticism

Aestheticism as a movement in the arts developed in England in the late nineteenth century, but somewhat earlier in other countries, such as

France, where it had its roots. The aestheticist dictum is "art for art's sake," meaning that an artwork need only be beautiful (well made) to be worthy of admiration. In other words, a work of art did not need to have any obvious social value to be great. So, for example, if an artist wished to depict the life of a criminal, as long as he or she did it well and accurately, the work of art was valuable. Also, if an artist simply wished to make a work of art, treating a subject that would not necessarily ennoble its audience, then that was fine, as long as the work was well-done. If this sounds like a reasonable formula for art, it is. Yet, aesthetes, or followers of aestheticism, caused a stir in England at the time because during the Victorian era the English developed a taste for art with a strong social quotient. They liked their art to be obviously ennobling. They wanted art to be morally instructive, for example, in which the good was clearly distinguished from the bad, the bad was always punished, and the good was always rewarded.

A further problem with aestheticism from the point of view of traditional, more conservative Victorians was that aesthetes took their principles very seriously, some to an extreme, and flaunted them. For example, the scholar most responsible for propagating aestheticist views in England, Walter Pater, wrote works proclaiming that the enjoyment, cultivation, and experience of beauty and exquisite sensation was one of the most important human pursuits of all. He wrote these rather extravagant ideas down, most famously, in the conclusion to a book entitled *The Renaissance.* Pater's followers, aesthetes, were, of course, dandies. They dressed beautifully, spoke beautifully, and enjoyed conversations about the best of art and decoration past and present.

Pater, an Oxford don, influenced Wilde while he was a student at Oxford. Not that Wilde's interests and life can be explained solely with reference to dandyism and Aestheticism, but these formations did, nonetheless, make their mark on Wilde.

Critical Overview

Many of the more serious critics of Wilde's day either ignored or were sparing in their praise of *An Ideal Husband*. By the time the play was staged, Wilde had many enemies, both major and minor. This was the result of his years as a dandy and his entire adult life as a cutting wit. On the one hand, he was thought frivolous and immoral; on the other, his wit often had as its target the very critics who were reviewing his work.

The critics of Wilde's time who were not impressed by the play thought it like its author: frivolous and lacking substance. Printed the day after the play opened, the review in London's major newspaper, *The Times,* is a case in point. An excerpt reads as follows:

> *An Ideal Husband* was brought out last night with a similar degree of success to that which has attended Mr. Wilde's previous productions. It is a similar degree of success due to similar causes. For *An Ideal Husband* is marked by the same characteristics as *Lady Windermere's Fan* and *A Woman of No Importance*. There is a group of well-dressed women and men on the stage, talking a strained, inverted, but rather amusing idiom, while the

action, the dramatic motive, of the play springs form [sic] a conventional device of the commonest order of melodrama. Mr. Wilde's ingenuity is verbal; there is none of this quality expended upon his plot and very little upon his characters, most of whom have caught the author's trick of phrase.

Still, negative reviews were far fewer for *An Ideal Husband* than for the previous two social comedies (named above) because by now critics hesitated to fly in the face of public opinion. No matter what they wrote, Wilde's comic plays had long runs and his supporters and audiences loved them.

Once Wilde was imprisoned, theaters ceased staging his plays for a time. But, within a decade or so, *An Ideal Husband* could be seen again. Reviews of these productions concentrated less on whether the plays deserved to be staged and more on the quality of the given production: Had the play been well directed? Well acted?

What would take more time to develop is academic scholarship on Wilde. With the exception of one or two studies, Wilde and his works did not begin receiving serious scholarly attention until the last decades of the twentieth century. A number of factors contributed to this academic interest: Wilde's wise analysis of late-Victorian culture was in accord with the prevailing view of the era; an interest in how Irish writers worked with and against the rules and canon of British literature became a subject of interest; and the developing fields of gender, sexuality, and gay and lesbian studies looked with interest on writers such as Wilde.

In general, critics consider Wilde's last comedy his best. In *The Importance of Being Earnest*, Wilde finally wrote what most critics think he should have written all along, namely a pure comedy of manners. There is no "social" plot to *The Importance of Being Earnest* and no melodrama.

Even as many of Wilde's works are considered very good works of art, he is as important for *who he was* in both public and private life as for what he wrote. This is appropriate, because to the aesthete, the art of living is what matters most. Mrs. Cheveley puts it this way: "The art of living. The only really Fine Art we have produced in modern times."

What Do I Read Next?

- The play *The Importance of Being Earnest* (1896) is Wilde's comedic masterpiece; it premiered a month after *An Ideal Husband* in 1895.

- *The Happy Prince and Other Tales* (1888) is Wilde's much admired first book of fairy tales.

- *Translations* (1981) is a play by the well-known Irish playwright Brian Friel. It takes place in 1833, dramatizing Britain's project of mapping Ireland and, in the process, substituting English names for the original Gaelic ones.

- The conclusion to *The Renaissance* (1873) by Walter Pater conveys the aestheticist creed that so impressed Wilde.

- Like Wilde's *The Importance of Being Earnest, The Way of the World* (1700) by William Congreve is said to be one of the finest and funniest comedies of manners ever written in English.

- Literary scholar Terry Eagleton's forays into fiction include a play about Oscar Wilde, *Saint Oscar* (1989). This humorous, erudite play explores the nature of Wilde's art and place in British society.

- The Norwegian Henrik Ibsen's most

famous "problem play," *A Doll's House* (1889), revolutionized European theater at the end of the nineteenth century. It set a new serious standard for playwrights, moving away from the fantastical entertainments of melodrama in favor of a new social realism in which social and political problems of the day were addressed. *A Doll's House* takes on the issue of the "New Woman."

- *Patience* (1881) is a comedic operetta about aesthetes and dandies by the famed Victorian musical theater duo W. S. Gilbert and Arthur Sullivan.

Sources

Belford, Barbara, "A Broken Line," in *Oscar Wilde: A Certain Genius,* Random House, 2000, p. 233.

Eagleton, Terry, Introduction, in *Saint Oscar, and Other Plays,* Blackwell Publishers, 1997.

Hall, Peter, "A Warm, Impossible Love," in the *Guardian,* November 11, 1992, Features Page, p. 4.

Nichols, Mark, "*An Ideal Husband*—The Wit and The Legend," in *The Importance of Being Oscar,* St. Martin's Press, 1983, pp. 91, 138.

Review of *An Ideal Husband,* in the *Times* (London), January 4, 1895, p. 7.

Wilde, Oscar, *An Ideal Husband,* in *The Plays of Oscar Wilde,* Random House, 1932.

Further Reading

Ellmann, Richard, *Oscar Wilde,* Alfred A. Knopf, 1988.

> This work is currently the most thorough and definitive biography of Wilde. In it, students of Wilde can read in minute detail about the author's life and career.

Holland, Vyvyan, *Oscar Wilde,* Thames and Hudson, 1960.

> This is a brief, informative book on the life of Wilde by his son, with photographs of Wilde, family, friends, and other notables. Holland corrects what he believes are inaccuracies in the major biographies of Wilde, such as those written by Frank Harris and Richard Ellmann.

Raby, Peter, ed., *The Cambridge Companion to Oscar Wilde,* Cambridge University Press, 1997.

> This collection by several authors on different aspects of Wilde's career and works contains many informative, recent essays. For example, one essay explores Wilde's four comedic plays as a group, and another compares Wilde's dramatic techniques to those of other major

playwrights of the time.

Roditi, Edouard, *Oscar Wilde,* New Directions, 1986.

> Most recent books on Wilde by literary scholars tend to focus on narrow, specialized subjects. Roditi's study, however, is a broad, general exploration of Wilde's art. As such, it is very useful for students looking for a general introduction to Wilde.

San Juan, Epifanio, Jr., *The Art of Oscar Wilde,* Princeton University Press, 1967.

> Like Roditi's study of Wilde, this scholarly exploration of Wilde is a comprehensive, useful introduction to Wilde's work.

Lightning Source UK Ltd.
Milton Keynes UK
UKHW021045110520
363093UK00001B/88